Germany ABCs

A Book About the People and Places of Germany

Country ABCs

Written by Sarah Heiman
Illustrated by Jason Millet

Germany Advisors:

Daniel Baron
German Teacher, Edina High School
Edina, Minnesota

Ruth Wassermann, Ph.D.
Heidelberg, Germany

Reading Advisor:

Lauren A. Liang, M.A.
Literacy Education, University of Minnesota
Minneapolis, Minnesota

PICTURE WINDOW BOOKS
Minneapolis, Minnesota

Editor: Peggy Henrikson
Designer: Nathan Gassman
Page production: Picture Window Books
The illustrations in this book were prepared digitally.

Picture Window Books
5115 Excelsior Boulevard
Suite 232
Minneapolis, MN 55416
1-877-845-8392
www.picturewindowbooks.com

Printed in the United States of America.

Library of Congress Cataloging-in-Publication Data
Heiman, Sarah, 1955–
Germany ABCs : a book about the people and places of Germany /
written by Sarah Heiman ; illustrated by Jason Millet.
p. cm. — (Country ABCs) Includes index.
Summary: An alphabetical exploration of the people, geography, animals, plants,
history, and culture of Germany.
ISBN 1-4048-0020-4 (hardcover)
ISBN 1-4048-0352-1 (softcover)
1. Germany—Description and travel—Juvenile literature. 2. Germany—Social life
and customs—Juvenile literature. [1. Germany. 2. Alphabet.] I. Millet, Jason, ill.
II. Title. III. Series.
DD17 .H54 2003
943—dc21
2002006276

German words are in *italics*, except where they have been accepted into the
English language or are proper nouns. In German, all nouns are capitalized.

Guten Tag! (GOO-ten TAHK)

That means "Good day!" in German. The country of Germany is in the northern part of central Europe. More than 83 million people live there. Germany ranks 12th in world population.

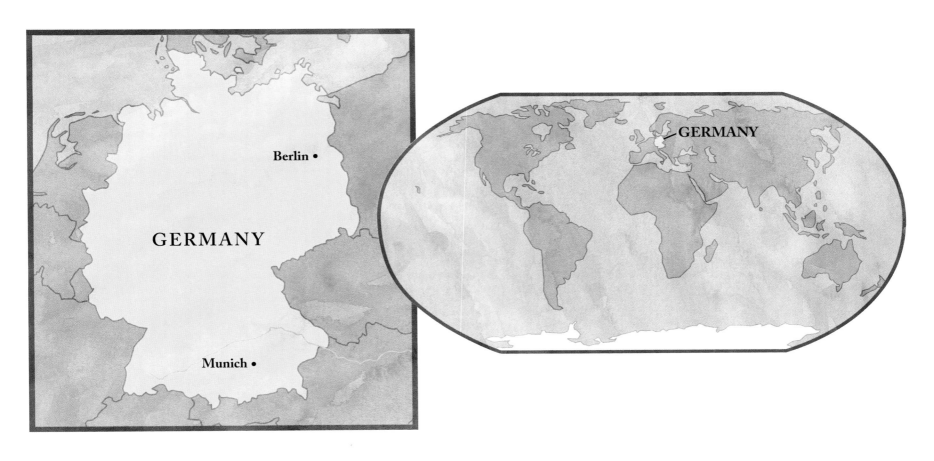

A is for author.

Two of the world's most famous authors are the German brothers Jakob and Wilhelm Grimm. In 1812, they collected and wrote down stories that had been passed down from parents to children for hundreds of years. These stories became known as Grimms' Fairy Tales.

Among the Grimms' Fairy Tales are "Little Red Riding Hood" and "Hansel and Gretel."

B is for Black Forest.

Forests cover much of Germany. The Black Forest is in the southwestern part of the country. The fir trees growing on the hillsides are so dark that they look black from far away.

C is for chancellor (CHAN-suh-lur).

Germany's chancellor is like the president of the United States or the prime minister of Canada. He is the head of Germany, a republic of 16 states.

In a republic, people are elected to make decisions for the whole country.

The German Parliament, like the United States Congress, is made up of two groups of people. People in the Bundestag make the laws, and people in the Bundesrat represent the states.

D is for dog.

Some of the most popular dog breeds came from Germany.
Among them are the dachshund, rottweiler, and German shepherd.

Ee

E is for euro (YOOR-oh).

In 2002, Germany and 12 other European countries started to use the same kind of money, called the euro. This means that when you travel through Europe, you don't have to get different money for every country you visit. The sign for the euro is €.

8

F is for flag.

The German flag was adopted in 1949. It has three stripes—black, red, and gold. Some say the colors came from Germany's ancient coat of arms. The flag stands for German unity, or oneness.

G is for Glockenspiel
(GLOCK-uhn-shpeel).

The Glockenspiel in the city of Munich is like a giant music box that is part of a bell tower. Inside the Glockenspiel, hammers strike bells to make music.

The Glockenspiel plays two different shows. In one show, painted copper figures dance and turn. They celebrate the end, in 1517, of a terrible sickness called the Black Plague. In the other show, painted knights on horseback fight with lances to celebrate a famous jousting event in 1568.

Hh

H is for houses.

Most Germans living in cities have apartments, because houses in Germany are very expensive. Tall, modern apartment buildings are often at the edges of large cities. In small towns, many older houses have tile roofs and are made of wood and stone.

I is for inventor.

An inventor is the first person to come up with an idea for something and also make it work. One important German inventor was Ferdinand Graf von Zeppelin. In 1909, he designed and made an airship that provided the world's first passenger air service.

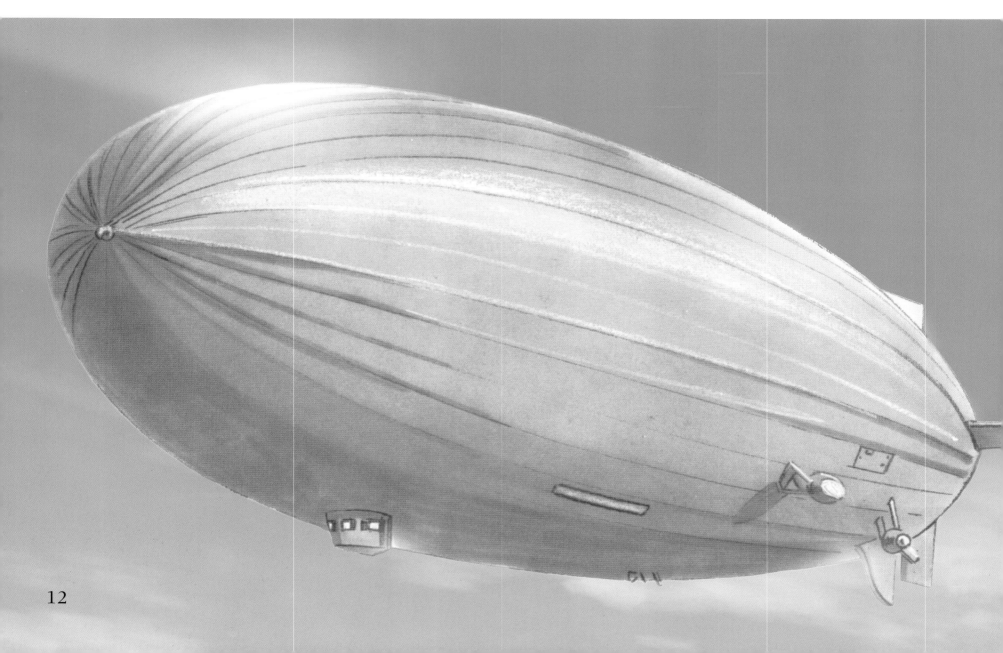

J is for Jacobikirche.

The Jacobikirche, or St. Jacob's Church, in Hamburg, Germany, was built in the 1300s. There are many such beautiful, old churches in Germany. Most Germans today follow the Christian religion and are either Protestant or Roman Catholic.

St. Jacob's has a famous pipe organ. Johann Sebastian Bach applied for the job of organist at St. Jacob's in 1720, but he wasn't hired. Bach is now known as one of the greatest musicians and composers of all time.

K is for Karneval (KAR-nuh-vahl).

Karneval is a season of street parties and costume balls that is celebrated in many parts of Germany. Every year it begins on November 11 at 11:11 in the morning and continues for three months. People wear masks or costumes, dance in the streets, and enjoy parades.

14

L is for lederhosen (LAY-dur-hoh-zuhn).

Lederhosen are short leather pants worn on special occasions by boys and men in parts of southern Germany. Girls and women wear a traditional dress called a dirndl (DURN-dul), which is often worn with a white apron.

M is for music.

Germany is the birthplace of many great musicians. Johann Sebastian Bach, Ludwig van Beethoven, and Johannes Brahms are three whose music has been played for hundreds of years.

Ludwig van Beethoven

Who	When	Famous Works
Johann Sebastian Bach	1685–1750	Brandenburg Concertos
Ludwig van Beethoven	1770–1827	Ninth Symphony
Johannes Brahms	1833–1897	Brahms' Lullaby

N is for nutcracker.

For hundreds of years, German craftsmen have carved wooden nutcrackers in the shapes of kings, soldiers, and villagers.

O is for Oktoberfest.

Oktoberfest is the world's largest festival, and it lasts for 16 days. It has been held nearly every October since 1810 in Munich. During the celebration, people listen to folk music, watch parades and dancing, and eat traditional German foods such as pretzels and bratwurst.

P p

P is for printing press.

A German named Johannes Gutenberg invented the printing press in the 1450s. Before that, books were written by hand. This took a long time. There weren't many books, and books cost a lot. Printing presses could make lots of books fast. These books cost less, so more people could buy them.

Q is for Quadriga (kwah-DREE-ga).

The Quadriga is a copper sculpture of four horses pulling a chariot driven by the winged goddess of peace. It sits on top of the famous stone monument called the Brandenburg Gate in Berlin, Germany's capital city.

R is for Rhine River.

The Rhine is Germany's longest and busiest river. Cruise ships and barges travel up and down the river past castles, churches, vineyards, and forests. One part of the Rhine Valley has more castles than any other river valley in the world.

21

S is for soccer.

Many Germans play soccer and watch it on television. They have neighborhood, school, and regional teams, as well as a national team. Other popular sports in Germany are tennis, biking, hiking, and skiing.

T is for transportation.

Germany is known for its good transportation systems. Trains are known for being on time. Germany's superhighway, the Autobahn, has no speed limit in some parts. Drivers can go as fast as they want.

23

U is for unity.

In 1945, after World War II, East Germany broke away from West Germany and became a separate country. The East German government wouldn't let people cross the border into West Germany to see family and friends. Finally, on October 3, 1990, East and West Germany were united again.

October 3 is Unity Day, a national holiday.

V is for vineyard.

Germany has over 250,000 acres (101,250 hectares) of vineyards. That's enough vineyards to cover 192,000 football fields. The grapes grown in these vineyards are used to make both white and red wines. Vineyards are especially common in the Rhine River Valley.

Ww

W is for wurst.

Wurst is the German word for sausage, and the word is now used in English, too. Bratwurst is a popular sausage in the United States. Germany produces more than 1,500 kinds of wurst.

26

X is for eXports.

Vehicles are one of Germany's most important exports. Others are farm machinery, foods, and computer and electrical parts.

Some German Cars Exported to North America

• Audi
• BMW
• Mercedes Benz
• Porsche
• Volkswagen

Y is for yes—*ja* (YAH).

The German word for "yes" is *ja*.

Other common words and phrases in German are:

German	Pronunciation	English
nein	NINE	no
danke	DAHNK-uh	thank you
hallo	HAHL-oh	hello
auf Wiedersehen	owf VEE-dur-zayn	good-bye

Z is for Zugspitze (TZOOG-shpit-zuh).

The Zugspitze is Germany's highest mountain peak. Tourists can get to the top by railway or cable car. Then they can look out over the snowy peaks of the big mountain range called the Bavarian Alps.

Make a *Schultüte* (cone of treats)!

On the first day of first grade, German parents give their children a large paper cone called a *Schultüte* (SHOOL-too-tuh). It is filled with candies, pencils, erasers, and other treats. The gift comes with a wish for the children to have a good and successful school year. Children of any age can enjoy a *Schultüte!* Here's how to make your own. You will need a friend to help you tape your cone.

What You Need

Newspaper
A large, square sheet of tagboard or poster board
Craft items such as glitter, lace, buttons, sequins, or ribbon
Glue
Colored markers

Tape
Sheets of colored tissue paper
Small treats such as stickers, candies, and school supplies
Ribbon

What to Do

1. Put the newspaper on the floor or a table, and lay the tagboard on top.

2. Glue craft items to the tagboard, and add pictures and patterns with markers. Leave about 1 inch (2½ centimeters) on the left and right sides undecorated. (This is where you will tape your cone together.)

3. Let the glue dry, then turn the tagboard over so the decorated side faces down.

4. Take the lower right corner and roll it up toward the upper left corner. Lap one edge over the other, leaving enough undecorated area to tape them together. (The top will overlap more than the bottom.) This will form a cone shape. Hold your cone while someone tapes the edges together.

5. Line the cone with tissue paper. Leave some of it sticking out of the top.

6. Fill the cone with treats.

7. Use your ribbon to tie the tissue paper closed at the top.

8. Enjoy your *Schultüte* and your successful year!

Fast Facts

Official name:	Federal Republic of Germany
Capital:	Berlin
Official language:	German
Population:	83,029,536
Area:	137, 826 square miles (356,970 square kilometers)
Highest point:	Zugspitze, 9,724 feet (2,964 meters)
Lowest point:	Freepsum Lake, 6.6 feet (2 meters) below sea level
Type of government:	federal republic
Head of government:	chancellor
Major industries:	construction, manufacturing
Natural resources:	iron ore, coal, copper, timber
Major agricultural products:	potatoes, wheat, barley, sugar
Chief exports:	automobiles, electrical machinery and appliances, chemical products
National flower:	centaurea or knapweed

Fun Facts

• The Neuschwanstein castle in southern Germany was the model for the castle in the Walt Disney movie *Sleeping Beauty*.

• The people of Hamburg are called Hamburgers.

• The first cuckoo clock was made in 1750 by a German farmer named Franz Anton Ketterer.

• Gummi Bears were invented in Germany.

Glossary

chancellor (CHAN-suh-lur)—a title sometimes used for the leader of a country

composer (kuhm-POH-zer)—the writer of a piece of music

concerto (kuhn-CHAIR-toh)—a piece of music for an orchestra with solo parts for a particular instrument

dirndl (DURN-dul)—a full skirt or dress, often worn with a white apron in Germany

jousting (JOW-sting)—fighting between two knights on horseback with long spears called lances

lederhosen (LAY-dur-hoh-zuhn)—short leather pants, often with suspenders

republic (ri-PUHB-lik)—a kind of government where the people elect a small group of people to make decisions for the whole; also the word for a country with that kind of government

symphony (SIM-fuh-nee)—a piece of music written for an orchestra

unity (YOO-nih-tee)—togetherness. When two separate things join together into one, there is unity.

To Learn More

At the Library

Gray, Shirley W. *Germany.* Minneapolis: Compass Point Books, 2002.

Kimmel, Eric A. *Seven at One Blow: A Tale from the Brothers Grimm.* New York: Holiday House, 1998.

McDermott, Dennis. *The Golden Goose.* New York: Morrow Junior Books, 2000.

Salas, Laura Purdie. *Germany.* Mankato, Minn.: Bridgestone Books, 2002.

On the Web

FactHound offers a safe, fun way to find Web sites related to this book. All of the sites on FactHound have been researched by our staff.

www.facthound.com

1. Visit the FactHound home page.
2. Enter a search word related to this book, or type in this special code: 1404800204.
3. Click the FETCH IT button.

Your trusty FactHound will fetch the best Web sites for you!

Index